KNOW THE FACTS

PERSONAL SAFETY

Judith Anderson

WAYLAND

First published in 2008
by Wayland

Copyright © Wayland 2008

Wayland
338 Euston Road
London NW1 3BH

Wayland Australia
Level 17/207 Kent Street
Sydney, NSW 2000

Series editor: Nicola Edwards
Consultant: David Ferguson
Designer: Jason Anscomb
Picture researcher: Kathy Lockley

All the photographs of young people have been posed by models. The author and publisher would like to thank the
models, and the following for allowing their pictures to be reproduced in this publication:
Cover: Wishlist Images; all inside photographs by Wishlist Images except: Stephen Frink Collection/Alamy: 12; Hill
Street Studios/Blend Images/Corbis: 26; Imagebroker/Alamy: 20; Nick North/Corbis: 4; Andersen Ross/Blend
Images/Corbis: 26; Ian Townsley/Alamy: 10; Janine Wiedel/Photofusion Photo Library: 18.

British Library Cataloguing in Publication Data

Anderson, Judith (Judith Mary)
   Personal safety. - (Know the facts)
   1. Offenses against the person - Prevention - Juvenile
   literature 2. Accidents - Prevention - Juvenile literature
   3. Safety education - Juvenile literature
   I. Title
   613.6

ISBN: 978 0 7502 5388 8

Printed in China

Wayland is a division of Hachette Children's Books,
an Hachette Livre UK company.
www.hachettelivre.co.uk

CONTENTS

HOW SAFE ARE YOU?

We all like to think we know how to stay safe. After all, most of the time we manage to cross the road successfully, boil a kettle without scalding ourselves and walk home without being mugged. But each year thousands of people do get hurt. They probably thought that they were safe until it was too late.

Young people at risk

When it comes to personal safety, children and young people can be especially vulnerable. For example, the statistics on pedestrian casualties below show that boys and girls aged 11-13 are most at risk. This is because these children are often starting at a different school, travelling independently for the first time and coping with all sorts of new hazards, such as crossing a road in the dark.

However, personal safety is not just about avoiding road traffic accidents. It is about learning to recognize, assess and manage all sorts of potential danger, whether in the home, out and about, with friends, online or on your own.

It's a Fact

- Most pedestrian accidents occur between 3 and 4 pm on a weekday, when school ends.
- An 11 year old boy is almost twice as likely as a 10 year old to be killed or seriously injured in a road accident.
- The pedestrian casualty rate for girls is highest at age 12.

New experiences

Try making a list of all the new things you have done over the past year. Think about travel, independence at home, playing sport, being with friends. Has anyone spoken to you about the dangers involved? Are you confident that you know how to stay safe?

Most young people want and need more independence as they get older.

WHAT'S THE PROBLEM?

'My mum says I'm not allowed to hang out in the street with my friends after school. I'm eleven years old and I don't want to stay in all the time. It's boring at home.'

Most parents worry about their child's safety. They think about traffic accidents and muggers and bullies and they need to feel confident that you are able to keep yourself out of danger. If you want more freedom, try talking to your mum about what you want to do, where you want to do it and who you will be with. Always agree a time when you will be home, and stick to it. Don't change your plans or go to someone's house without telling her first.

One way to see your friends away from home is to join a club where you can play sport or do other activities that will stop you feeling bored and give you more independence.

RISK

No one wants to get hurt. Yet there is a certain amount of risk in many of our daily activities. Imagine you are playing a game of basketball. You know that if you run to intercept the ball you may collide with another player. You also know that serious injury is quite rare in a basketball game. So if you want the ball you may decide it is a risk you are prepared to take.

HAVE YOUR SAY

"I like taking risks. It gives me a buzz."

"Taking risks is part of growing up, isn't it? That's how people learn!"

"I never walk home from town on my own. It's too risky."

"My dad won't let me light candles in my room. He says they're a fire risk."

Assessing risk

If we wanted to avoid risk altogether then we would probably never get out of bed in the morning. So, in order to make it through our day successfully and without injury, we must constantly carry out risk assessment. This means weighing up the dangers that we know about, looking for hidden dangers, and considering how well we might cope if disaster strikes.

Sometimes risk assessment happens in a split second. Sometimes, however, if we are doing something we haven't done before, we need to step back and take a little longer to think through the potential danger. **Remember, if you don't know what the dangers are, you won't be able to carry out an effective risk assessment.**

This gymnast wants to do a handstand on the top bar. She has never done one before. She knows that if she falls, she might hurt herself. But she has practised doing handstands on the lower bar. Her coach thinks she is ready, and is standing by. She decides to go for it!

What Would you do?

Your brother has thrown your shoe up onto the garage roof. Do you:

a) climb out of an upstairs window and onto the roof to get it;

b) abandon your shoe;

c) fetch a ladder?

Turn to page 47 for the answers.

Road accidents are one of the most common causes of injury and death amongst children and young people. Sometimes this is because young people themselves take unnecessary risks, such as crossing between two parked cars or weaving in and out of traffic on their bikes. However, sometimes accidents happen because children are not aware of the risks that adult drivers take.

If you have to cross a road from between parked cars, remember that drivers and cyclists won't see you until you step into the road.

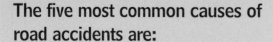

It's a Fact

The five most common causes of road accidents are:

- a driver's failure to judge another person's path or speed;
- careless or reckless behaviour;
- inattention;
- looking but failing to see;
- excessive speed.

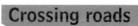

Crossing roads

Many children who are involved in road accidents are not walking across a road, they are running. If you are in a hurry, you are less likely to be aware of other road-users. Always stop, look both ways and listen for hidden traffic before you cross a road. Pedestrian crossings provide a safer place to cross but never assume that drivers will stop until they have actually come to a halt. You might be able to see them but they might not have seen you.

Cycling in traffic

Do you know your highway code? There are standard signals that all cyclists should know before they ride on the road. However, a cyclist also needs to understand the signals a motor vehicle uses. Always keep an eye on the indicator lights and brake lights of the car in front. Never cycle too close to a vehicle as it may turn or stop unexpectedly. Remember, many motorists do not look out for cyclists and may not know that you are there. Also, avoid using ear phones while cycling; you won't hear traffic approaching from behind.

Is your bike safe?

Don't take risks with a bike that isn't safe. You need to make sure that your brakes and lights are working properly. Check the gears and tyres, too. Seat height is also important. If your feet can't touch the ground then you won't be able to stop without falling off.

Help yourself

Be safe when you're cycling or crossing a road.

- Make yourself as visible as possible. Wear bright colours. Stick reflective strips on your back pack or your cycle helmet.
- Never run across a road. If it isn't safe to walk, it isn't safe to cross.
- Always use bike lights or a torch in the dark.
- Never assume that a car driver has seen you.

Over half of all cycling injuries are head injuries. Always wear a helmet!

IN YOUR HOME

More accidents happen in the home than anywhere else. It is hard to believe, until you begin to list all the different hazards that our homes contain. Boiling water, chemicals for cleaning, electrical equipment, stairs, cookers, fireplaces, knives, scissors... All have the potential to do serious harm to you or to someone else in your family.

Fire

Nearly half of all accidental child deaths occur in house fires. House fires are most commonly started in the kitchen or as a result of a burning match or cigarette. Never leave candles, incense or cigarettes burning unattended. Electrical appliances also cause fires. Make sure you always use the manufacturer's recommended socket or plug and switch off after use.

Talk through any fire procedures with your parents or carers. Are there smoke alarms fitted in your home? Do you know what to do if there is a fire?

WHAT'S THE PROBLEM?

'My brother, who is 18, smokes in his bedroom. I'm worried he'll start a fire. What should I do?'

Smoking in a bedroom is particularly dangerous. If the smoker falls asleep, the burning ash can quickly start a fire. Try talking to your brother, and explain your fears. If he won't stop smoking, then a few basic safety precautions will limit the risk. Ask him to use a deep, fireproof ashtray (dropping ash in a waste paper bin is a bad idea), and see if he will agree to smoke in a chair rather than on his bed. Ask for a smoke alarm to be installed outside his room.

In the kitchen

Hot things, sharp things - kitchens are full of them. Yet learning how to cook and keep things clean is an important step on the road to independence. Safety in the kitchen is about thinking ahead. **Think** before you turn on the heat. Is there anything (tea towels, kettle flexes) you need to move away first? **Think** before you lift up that hot pan. Should you use an oven glove? **Think** before you use that sharp knife. Are your hands wet or slippery?

Consider others

Even if you know that it is not a good idea to drink bleach or put your fingers in your hair straighteners, do remember that other members of your family may not. And if you cannot deal with a hazard yourself, make sure you tell others about it. Always check that anything potentially dangerous (such as medicines, chemicals, knives, needles) is kept out of a younger child's reach.

What Would you do? ?

There is a piece of bread stuck in the toaster. Do you:

(a) fish it out with a knife;
(b) turn off the power at the socket and tell an adult that there is a problem;
(c) have cereal for breakfast instead?

Turn to page 47 for the answers.

When cutting or chopping, make sure that you angle the knife away from your fingers.

WATER SAFETY

Many fun activities take place on, in or near water. However, whether you are an accomplished swimmer or merely paddling in your local stream, you need to be aware of your own limitations. You also need to understand the dangers of the particular water environment in which you find yourself.

Learn to swim

Being able to swim is no guarantee of safety in water, but it is a vital first step. You don't need to be a stylish swimmer and you don't need to be fast, but if you can learn how to stay afloat you significantly increase your chances of survival. If you cannot swim, always wear a proper lifejacket when doing water activities of any kind, even if you are just sitting in a rowing boat.

Help yourself

Be safe when you're in and around water.

- Learn to swim.
- Wear a lifejacket at all times on a boat, even if you can swim.
- Don't rely on water rings or other swimming 'aids'.
- Obey warning flags on beaches.
- Never swim alone.
- Know the depth of the water and be aware of any obstacles beneath the surface.
- Insist on adult supervision of younger children.

Scuba divers never dive alone, and use an agreed set of hand signals to let each other know that they are OK.

Hidden danger

Those who can swim often overlook water's hidden dangers. Do you know how deep it is? Are there any obstacles such as rocks or thick weed lying beneath the surface? Is there a strong current or undertow? Don't rely on sight alone. If you're not sure, don't risk it.

Buddy up

Never swim or do any kind of water-based sport alone. However, trying to keep a non-swimmer afloat may put you in danger, so first make sure that everyone else with you can swim or is wearing a lifejacket. Don't let anyone leave you with young children near water - they can drown in as little as a few centimetres and should always be supervised by a responsible adult.

It's a Fact ✓

- Nearly 90 per cent of those who drown in boating accidents are not wearing a lifejacket.
- Children aged 0-4 drown mainly in buckets and baths.
- Children aged 5-14 drown mainly in residential swimming pools and open water such as lakes and rivers.

A SPORTING CHANCE

Sport is about keeping fit, having fun and challenging ourselves to go further, or faster or higher. No sport is entirely free of risk and that, for many, is part of its appeal. However, this risk can be managed and the danger significantly reduced with a little preparation.

A simple warm-up routine will include stretching, bending and jogging on the spot.

Warming up

Too many sports injuries occur because young people don't prepare their bodies properly. Making time for a simple warm-up routine that's right for your sport will help you avoid damage to your muscles, ligaments and joints.

Joining a club

Some sports are more dangerous than others. Always wear the recommended safety equipment and follow recognised safety procedures. Joining a club is a great way to develop your interest in a sport without compromising on safety, as clubs usually offer tuition, advice and the loan of any expensive equipment, as well as other people to practise with.

HAVE YOUR SAY

"I always stretch before I run. If I don't I get a stitch or cramp or something."

"I wear a gum shield when I play rugby. I don't want to get my teeth knocked out!"

What's right for you?

Most people enjoy a challenge, but no one should feel pressured into doing anything they don't want to do. When you are faced with something new, ask yourself if you feel comfortable with the level of risk. Have you prepared yourself properly and received appropriate instruction? Do you trust your equipment? If something goes wrong, are there people around who will know how to help you?

These canoeists are dressed appropriately, in an exhilarating and challenging environment.

WHAT'S THE PROBLEM?

'I used to love trampolining but my best friend damaged his neck and now I'm worried that the same thing will happen to me.'

No sport is free from risk. If you want to carry on trampolining, try to minimise this risk by taking a class at the right level for you, always warming up properly, and only trying new moves with the guidance and supervision of a trained instructor.

You could also talk to your friend about why he thinks he injured himself, and learn from his mistake. Let skill and confidence build gradually. Above all, enjoy it!

EMERGENCY!

We cannot eliminate all risk from our lives. No matter how careful we are, sometimes things go wrong. However, if you or someone else gets hurt it is vital to limit the damage as much as possible. Knowing what to do in an emergency can make all the difference.

Always be prepared

When you go out with your friends, check that one of you has a phone that is fully charged and working. Then, if something does go wrong, you can call for help.

If you are doing a physical activity such as mountain biking, you might want to keep a small first aid kit with you, containing dressings for cuts. Taking a basic first aid course is an excellent way for everyone to prepare for accidents and emergencies.

WHAT'S THE PROBLEM?

'I don't want to tell my friends that I have epilepsy. They might think I'm a freak.'

You're not a freak. Epilepsy is surprisingly common. Your friends may have someone in their family with the same condition. Telling them about it may make them feel trusted, and they will probably be keen to find out more. Most importantly though, your friends need to know what to do if you have a seizure. Then they can help you, instead of feeling helpless themselves.

Before you leave home, make sure you have everything you need with you, such as money and a phone. If you have an allergy or a medical condition such as diabetes or epilepsy, don't forget your medicine and instructions for others in case you become ill.

Knowing how to put someone into the recovery position can save their life if they are unconscious. However, once the emergency services have been called, follow any instructions they give you and stay with the person until they arrive.

Make sure your friends know if you suffer from a dangerous allergy or a condition such as asthma or epilepsy. Do they know what to do if you get into difficulties?

Dealing with injury

If someone is injured, the most important thing to do is to call or shout for help. Try to stay calm, and make sure that you are not in any danger yourself. The panel opposite explains what to do with different types of injury, but if you are not sure then stay with the injured person and wait for the emergency services to arrive so that you can tell them what happened.

Help yourself

If someone is hurt:

- Stay calm.
- Stay out of danger.
- Call the emergency services and wait for them to arrive.
- Do not give the injured person anything to eat or drink.
- If they are awake, ask them to stay still.
- **For burns:**
  Treat with cold running water until help arrives.
- **For bleeding:**
  Apply pressure to the wound. Raise up the affected part and support it until help arrives.
- **For loss of consciousness:**
  Roll the person very gently onto their side to keep their airway open.

DANGER SIGNS

DON'T RUN! KEEP OUT! DEEP WATER! COVER UP!
People do all sorts of crazy things. They fall off buildings, get carried out to sea, swallow harmful substances or suffer severe sun burn. Yet most of these disasters could be prevented if those concerned observed the warning signs.

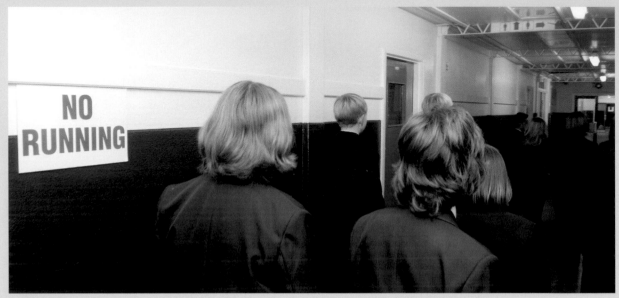
Perhaps there is a rule that you don't like. Think about it, talk about it, but don't just ignore it.

Reasons for rules

Of course, no one likes being told what they can't do. And sometimes it can seem as if parents, teachers or the police are being over-cautious.

It feels like a limit on freedom, and on fun. Why shouldn't I dive off that rock? Why can't I skate in the car park? Who says I can't light that firework?

HAVE YOUR SAY

"I don't need a signal to tell me when it is safe to cross the road."

"People only put up danger signs because they don't want to get sued."

However, even if you have considered the danger to yourself, have you thought about the risks to others? If you dive off a rock and hit your head, someone else will have to get into the water to rescue you. If you lose control of your skateboard, you may hit a pedestrian. If you light that firework it might explode in someone's face.

Remember, danger signs are there to protect you and those around you. Laws are made to keep you and others safe. If you decide to behave recklessly and someone else gets hurt then you are responsible.

Danger signs are there for a reason.
Never ignore them.

What Would you do?

A fair has arrived in the field on the far side of the railway line. The pedestrian bridge is a mile away. It is much quicker to climb the fence and hop across the track. Would you:

(a) cross the track carefully, looking both ways;
(b) walk the mile to the safe crossing;
(c) sprint over the tracks as quickly as possible?

Turn to page 47 for the answers.

PEER PRESSURE

Most people want to be part of a group or want to fit in. But sometimes being part of a group can be difficult. There is pressure to be fashionable, to be funny, to be cool. Someone who refuses to join in may find themselves excluded from the group. This pressure can lead to some difficult choices.

Dares

Has anyone ever dared you to do something? Dares are about getting someone else to take a risk. They can be fun, if everyone feels comfortable with the level of risk. However, sometimes you may feel pressured into doing something that you know is dangerous. Remember, the person daring you is probably too scared to do it themselves. If you are worried, just say 'No'.

No, thank you!

If someone smokes, drinks alcohol or takes drugs, they often want those around them to do it too. It makes whatever they are doing seem fun, or okay. It makes it a group activity. Saying 'No' to cigarettes, alcohol or other drugs isn't easy when your friends are pressurising you. But if your friends don't respect your wishes, are they good friends?

If you can confidently say 'No', your friends are less likely to put pressure on you next time.

WHAT'S THE PROBLEM?

'I'm too scared to go down the ramps at the bike park. They are really steep. But my friends say I can't go with them if I don't.'

Your friends can't tell you what to do, but if you are worried then maybe biking at the ramps isn't for you at the moment. That's okay. Tell your friends you'll see them at some other activity, or perhaps go along without your bike but with a camera instead. Taking pictures of them will give you a good reason to be there and your friends will like having a record of their achievements!

Take care of your skin in the sun. It's not cool to burn, and it isn't healthy either.

Looking good

The pressure to achieve a certain 'look' can be very strong. Who has the slimmest waist, the deepest suntan, the biggest muscles? But trying to change the way we are in order to conform to a particular body image may not be healthy. Excessive dieting, sunbathing or body building is extremely harmful. There are so many other ways to feel good about ourselves and like ourselves as we are.

Help yourself

Coping with peer pressure

- Be yourself.
- Choose friends who respect you for who you are.
- Avoid situations where others can bully you into doing something you don't want to do.
- Practise saying 'No'; rehearse your arguments or make a joke of it.
- Remember, if you say 'No' with confidence you may increase the respect of your peers.

BULLYING

A bully is a person who is repeatedly mean to someone or hurts them on purpose. Bullying behaviour includes making threats, sending nasty texts, physically hurting someone, telling lies about them, taking their stuff or deliberately ignoring them.

Being bullied

If you are being bullied, the first thing to remember is that it is not your fault. Bullies may try to make you feel that you are stupid or weak but this is all part of their bullying behaviour. The second thing to remember is that there are lots of people who can help you. Find someone you can trust. It might be your parents, or your teacher, or a good friend or someone at school who is a bit older than you. Tell them what has happened, and how you feel.

WHAT'S THE PROBLEM?

'An older girl at my school keeps telling me she will beat me up on my way home. I am really scared. None of my friends walk the same way as me.'

Don't feel you have to wait until this girl attacks you. Her threatening behaviour is bullying and you do not have to put up with it. Try talking to someone about what has been happening, and how it makes you feel. Is there a school counsellor or a teacher you can trust? The threats are being made at school and so the school has a responsibility to take action. You could also try telling this girl that you have made a record of every incident. If you show her that you are taking control she may decide to leave you alone.

Bullies are less likely to target people in groups.

If you are being bullied, don't bottle it up inside. You'll feel better, and stronger, if you tell somone you trust.

Help yourself

Get help to stop being bullied

- Don't keep it to yourself; tell someone you can trust.
- Write down the time, place and type of every bullying incident. This will make it easier for you to tell someone exactly what has been going on.
- Stay with friends or walk home in a group wherever possible, as bullies tend to target people who are on their own.
- If you have confided in someone but the bullying continues, don't give up. Tell someone else. Keep telling people until the bullying stops.

Make a difference

If you know of someone who is being bullied, you don't need to confront the bullies in order to help. Instead, tell a teacher or another responsible adult what you have seen. This isn't 'telling tales' — it is helping to stop cruel and damaging behaviour. You and your friends could ask the bullied person if they would like to join your group, as bullies often prefer to target those who are on their own.

WHO CAN YOU TRUST?

Being trustworthy means doing something when you say you are going to do it, being honest, considering someone else's needs and not letting someone else down. We all have to trust other people sometimes, and who we trust is very important.

Choosing the right person

If you are worried about something, the best thing you can do is tell someone. Friends are often good listeners, and sometimes just talking is enough to make you feel better. But if you are being bullied, or have a serious problem, you may need to talk to a person who can really change things for you. Adults such as teachers, counsellors, parents and doctors are usually on your side, wanting to help.

Keeping a secret

What if a friend tells you they have stopped eating because they want to lose weight, or they are taking drugs, and asks you to keep it a secret? This puts you in a very difficult position. On the one hand you don't want to break their trust, but on the other hand you know they are harming themselves. However, remember that your friend is not yet an adult. They are not fully responsible for their actions and neither are you. If they are hurting themselves or anyone else then you must tell a responsible adult.

HAVE YOUR SAY

"I trust my big sister. I can tell her anything."

"My counsellor says our chats are confidential. That means she won't tell anyone else what I say."

Trusting a stranger

Most of us have contact with strangers every single day. We sit next to them in the cinema, we queue with them at the bus stop, we speak to them in shops and cafes. No one should walk around in fear of strangers, because most of the time they are just like us. However, following a few simple rules will help you to stay safe.

- Never give out your address or phone number, in person or online, unless it is to a member of the emergency services.
- Stay in a crowd wherever possible.
- If you are lost or need help, approach someone in a position of responsibility such as a parent with young children or a shop assistant or a bus driver.
- Trust your instincts. If someone makes you feel uncomfortable, move away.

What Would you do?

A man approaches you in the street and asks if you would like a free haircut at a new hair salon he is promoting. You say yes and he asks for your name and address so that he can send you a voucher in the post. Do you:

(a) Give him your name and address;
(b) Ask to see some official ID;
(c) Refuse to give any personal details?

Turn to page 47 for the answers.

Counsellors are trained to listen and to help.

SAFETY IN NUMBERS

Everyone is more vulnerable when they are alone. It doesn't matter whether you are walking up a mountain or just walking home from the cinema. If something goes wrong, you'll need help. There really is safety in numbers.

Keeping in a group

When you are in a group of people you know, you are less likely to be picked on or bullied. Be especially careful after dark or late at night. If you are at a party or a club, wait for someone to come out with you, or leave early rather than leave alone. If you are doing an adventurous activity like mountain biking or orienteering it is a good idea to be with at least one other person. Then, if you get hurt, someone can stay with you while someone else fetches help.

Too many people?

Being in a group is never dangerous if people in the group behave sensibly. But it is a good idea to be careful in a large crowd. Don't allow yourself to be pushed off a crowded pavement, for example. Sometimes crowds can feel a bit threatening at a big public event such as a football game or a concert. If this is the case, you might feel more comfortable on the edge of the crowd, so that you can get away if you need to.

HAVE YOUR SAY

"I'm supposed to check that my phone is charged up before I go out."

"Me and my friends always meet at the end of my road. We like walking to school together!"

"I'm not allowed to cycle off-road unless my mates are with me."

WHAT'S THE PROBLEM?

'My friend promised she'd come home with me after a party but then she went off with someone else and left me on my own. My mum says next time she'll come and pick me up but I don't want her to - no one else's parents make such a fuss.'

Your mum just wants to make sure you get home safely. Perhaps if you can find someone more reliable than your friend to see you home, then your mum will feel reassured. But having your mum pick you up, even if it is embarrassing, is much better than walking home late in the evening on your own. Try talking to her about it. Maybe you can both agree that she will wait in the car until you come out, so that she doesn't have to come to the door. If you both have mobile phones, she could send you a text to let you know when she's there.

Wherever you go to have fun, whether it's an amusement park, a sports ground or a cimema, always make sure that someone at home knows where you are and that you know how to get home safely.

Keeping in touch

Whether you are on your own or in a group, letting others know where you are going and what you are doing is really important. Then, if something happens and you can't get home, people know how to find you. One of the easiest ways to keep in touch is to use a mobile phone. Remember though, a phone is no guarantee of safety. You won't always be able to get a signal, and if you get hurt you may not be able to use a phone anyway. There's also the risk that a mobile phone might get lost, or stolen. It's a good idea to carry a few coins with you, so that you can use a public phone if you need to.

ON YOUR WAY

Sometimes it just isn't possible to travel with someone you know. However, there are plenty of ways to stay safe when you travel alone. Whether you are walking, cycling or travelling on public transport, the first thing to do is tell a responsible adult. Let them know when you are leaving, how you are travelling and what time you expect to arrive at your destination.

Walking

If you have to walk alone, try to stick to busy streets with lots of other passers-by. Remember, it is better to be seen than to try to make yourself invisible. If it is dark, walk under streetlights and try to stay fairly close to other pedestrians. Make sure you can be seen by drivers. If you have to walk down a quiet street, or a poorly lit street, don't hide in the shadows but walk down the middle of the road if there is no traffic. This will give you confidence, and may put off any potential attackers.

Help yourself

Safety on the street

If you think you are being followed in the street:

- Don't try to hide down a side street or a footpath.
- Don't confront your pursuer.
- Make yourself as visible as possible to other road users.
- Walk quickly towards other pedestrians or go into a shop or other public building.
- Tell an adult what has happened.

On public transport

Again, follow the rule about safety in numbers. Try to sit with lots of other people. If the train or bus is empty, don't go and sit in a deserted carriage or on the top deck by yourself. Try to sit near the driver or the guard or ticket inspector. If someone approaches you on public transport and makes you feel uncomfortable for any reason, get up and move away but don't get off unless you can see other people at the bus stop or on the station platform.

Cars and taxis

Don't get into an unmarked taxi unless you know the driver well. Try to use properly registered cabs at all times. Never accept a lift from a stranger. If a car pulls up alongside, even to ask directions, do not lean in through the window but stand well back on the pavement.

If you are travelling alone on a bus, make sure you try to sit downstairs where the driver can see you.

What Would you do?

A train pulls into the station. The first carriage is quite full, the second carriage has one person in it and the third carriage is empty. Which one will you choose?

Turn to page 47 for the answer.

THEFT AND MUGGING

Thieves and muggers don't just rob people of their possessions; they cause huge distress to their victims. Children and young people in particular can seem like easy targets. However, taking a few simple precautions can significantly reduce your chances of being robbed or mugged.

Theft at school

Theft is an all too common problem in most schools. Unattended bags are a fact of life and not everyone has access to a safe locker during sports or gym lessons. However, you can minimise the risk to yourself by leaving items such as jewellery, purses and music players at home. If you need to take off your watch or earrings during sport, find out if there is somewhere safe to store them. Ask if you can leave valuables within sight of everyone during your lesson, in a designated part of the gym or on the sidelines of the playing field.

It's a Fact

- 11-16 year olds are more likely to be the victims of theft and street crime than any other age group.
- Most muggings happen in the street or on public transport in the evening between 6 pm and 11 pm.
- Items most likely to be stolen are wallets and purses, music players, mobile phones and jewellery.

Mugging

Mugging is a form of street crime in which the thief uses threats or violence to demand money and valuables from their victims. It is a frightening and shocking type of crime but you can reduce the risk of it happening to you by making sure that when you are out and about, your possessions are well hidden. Try also to stay in a group and avoid dimly lit areas and isolated places.

If you are mugged, just give the attacker your stuff and don't try to fight back.

HAVE YOUR SAY

"I had my wallet stolen out of my back pocket. Now I keep it in a pocket inside my jacket."

Don't make yourself a target. Keep phones and music players out of sight on the street.

Help yourself

Protect yourself against bicycle theft

- Half of all bicycles are stolen from home. Always leave your bike in a secure place, out of sight from the street.
- Get your bike tagged or security marked and make sure this is visible to deter thieves.
- When you are away from home, never leave your bike unlocked. Use a good quality lock, securing it through the frame to an immovable object.
- Never leave your bike in a quiet or dimly lit place – this just makes it easier for thieves.
- Try not to lock it in the same place on a regular basis to deter thieves stealing bikes 'to order'.

Your safety is far more important than your possessions. Running away or shouting and screaming are sometimes enough to put off an attacker, but whatever happens you must call the police straight away.

MOBILE PHONES

Mobile phones can make us all feel much more secure. With a mobile phone you can stay in touch, let people know where you are, and contact the emergency services if necessary. However, owning a mobile phone can create a new set of problems.

What does it cost?

Having a mobile phone often means you receive all sorts of messages asking you to sign up for new ring tones or enter competitions. Be aware that messages like these are usually trying to get you to spend money. How much does that ring tone cost? Will you be paying each time it plays? Remember too that some telephone numbers are premium rate numbers, designed to make maximum profit out of your call.

Anti-theft precautions

Make sure you register your phone with your service provider and keep a note of the serial IMEI number (usually on the back of the battery) and your own telephone number. With this information your service provider will be able to block all calls if your phone is stolen. It is also a good idea to mark your phone with an ultra-violet pen and keep the keypad locked when you are not using it. Never let a stranger use your mobile phone.

The best way to keep your phone safe is to make sure that you keep it out of sight wherever possible.

Bullying by phone

Texts, voicemail and video phone images are often used by bullies to intimidate or undermine people, because they are difficult to trace. However, you can still take control if you receive any nasty messages. You can change your number, tell your mobile phone service provider and, if the messages are threatening or persistent, tell the police. If someone is bullying you in this way they are breaking the law.

WHAT'S THE PROBLEM?

'Someone is sending me horrible texts, telling me I'm going to get hurt. I am really frightened.'

These messages are being sent by someone who gets a thrill out of frightening people. Don't be tempted to reply and only answer calls from a number you recognise. Tell an adult like your mum or a teacher, show them the messages and save them so that you have proof which you might decide to take to the police.

If your caller ID says 'number withheld' then call your mobile phone service provider as they will often provide advice about what to do next. However, one of the simplest ways to deal with this kind of bullying is to change your number and only give the new number to people you really trust.

Phone bullies are like any other bullies. If someone is sending you nasty messages, tell an adult you can trust and change your number.

KEEP IT PRIVATE!

The internet is a great way to communicate, find things out, play games and download music. It is a bit like a virtual playground. Nevertheless, every user needs to understand the risks. The internet has the potential to seriously threaten your safety and security.

Making it public

Instant messaging and social networking sites are fun and easy ways to keep in touch with your friends. However, do remember that anything you post on a public blog can be copied and forwarded without your permission. Do you really want total strangers to read your private thoughts or see a video clip of you doing a handstand? Of course you can always delete something from your own space or blog but by then it may be too late. Think very carefully before you post any images or personal information about yourself or others.

Don't let others pressure you into doing anything you're not comfortable with online.

It's a Fact ✓

- Anything you post in a public forum or chat room can be copied or altered and forwarded in a matter of seconds to anyone, all around the world.

Personal details

You wouldn't give out your full name and address to a bunch of strangers on the bus, would you? Treat the internet in the same way. Never give out any information about who you are, where you live, the name of your school or where you hang out to anyone who is not a friend you know face-

to-face, even if you are using a 'friends only' space. You don't want your personal details getting into the wrong hands.

Photos and video clips

Video sharing sites can be great fun but only if the person in the clip is genuinely happy to share their funny or embarrassing moment with the whole world. Remember too that photos and video clips can be cut and pasted or photoshopped into something that perhaps you hadn't intended and might feel very upset about.

Don't forget that pictures and clips can reveal a lot about you. For example, a picture of you in your school blazer makes it easy to identify your school.

Protecting your stuff

Passwords are essential for protecting your privacy online. However, try to use different passwords for different activities as this reduces the likelihood of someone else working it out. Remember too that your computer is vulnerable to viruses and hackers whenever you are logged on. Always make sure that your firewall is enabled and that you have up-to-date anti-virus software installed.

Help yourself

Keeping safe on the internet

It may seem like there are hundreds of dos and don'ts about protecting your privacy on the internet. Here is a checklist of some of the most important things to remember.

- Never give out personal details such as your full name, address or school on the internet.
- Always use a nickname.
- Use passwords wherever possible, and don't make them too obvious. A mix of letters and numbers is best. Don't share them with anyone - not even your best friend.
- Remember to tick the 'no pic forwarding' option on your settings page.
- Never open attachments or messages from people you don't know.
- Keep your firewall enabled and your anti-virus software up to date.

Never post anything that you wouldn't want the whole world to see.

INTERNET FRIENDS

Think about your friends from school or your neighbourhood for a moment. Why do you get on with them? Maybe they are the same age as you. Maybe they are kind, or funny, or perhaps you have shared lots of experiences together. Do you trust them? Why?

When you trust someone, you expect them to tell you the truth and to behave caringly towards you.

There is nothing wrong with making friends online. But do you know tham as well as friends you see every day or go to school with?

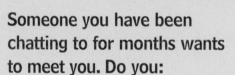

What Would you do?

Someone you have been chatting to for months wants to meet you. Do you:

(a) invite them over when your parents are at home;

(b) arrange to meet them in a public place;

(c) ask to see a picture of them first?

Turn to page 47 for the answers.

Who are you talking to?

Unfortunately it is very easy to lie on the internet. People can change their age, their sex and their interests without anyone knowing. They might do this to make themselves seem more exciting, but they might do it because they want to trick you into trusting them. Sex pests and paedophiles frequently pretend to be much younger in order to get children to chat to them. They may pretend to have the same interests, and even pretend to understand your problems in order to persuade you to give them personal information about yourself.

Talk to your parents about what you are doing online. Most of the time they just want to know that you are safe.

Be aware

If you are chatting to someone you haven't met in person, don't be persuaded to give them any personal information or post any images of yourself. Don't use a webcam either. Make sure you stay in a public forum. If someone asks you to move into a private area of a chat room, refuse and if anyone says something that makes you feel uncomfortable, block them immediately. Always tell an adult if this happens. It isn't your fault. There are some nasty people out there.

WHAT'S THE PROBLEM?

'Why do adults get so stressed about chat rooms?'

It can seem very unfair if your dad or your teacher gives you a hard time about chat rooms and other sites when you have made friends and enjoy contacting them in this way. But parents and teachers are there to protect you. They are aware of all the dangers and need to know that you are not giving out personal details that may make you vulnerable to others. It is always a good idea to talk things through with them; tell them what sites you visit and show them you are taking sensible precautions. However, if they still want to ban a particular site then do what they say. Logging on in secret makes you an easy target for those who want to abuse your trust.

HOME ALONE

When are you old enough to be left on your own? How do you feel about being alone in your home? Sometimes young people relish the prospect of being trusted by their parents or having the freedom to do what they like. But sometimes, being on your own can be a bit worrying, or frightening.

What does the law say?

Many countries don't have laws about the age at which a child can be left alone, as they recognise that there are so many different factors to take into account, such as the maturity of the child, the period of time involved, and the level of danger in the environment in which they have been left. But most countries agree that it is illegal to leave any child under the age of 16 if this puts them at risk. For example, it might be reasonable for a parent to leave a responsible eleven year old alone in the house for half an hour while they pop to the supermarket, but it would not be reasonable or safe to leave the same child alone while they go out for the night.

Some children enjoy a little independence. Others feel less confident.

HAVE YOUR SAY

"My mum says I can't babysit my five year old sister until I am fifteen."

"My mum tells our next door neighbour if she leaves me at home. It's embarrassing. I'm fourteen years old!"

Talk about it

If you know you are going to be at home alone for any length of time, talk to your parents or carers first. If you feel worried, tell them. Discuss what you would do if there was an emergency, or you felt frightened. Make sure you know where your parents or carers will be, when they will be back and how you can contact them. It is a good idea to have a list of useful numbers by the phone, including the emergency services and any other trusted adults who could help you.

Stay safe

Accidents are probably the greatest risk if you are home alone. Don't try to surprise your mum by cooking a three-course meal if you are not already a very experienced chef! Don't use electrical equipment unless it has been agreed first, and never use matches or lighters without an adult around.

Remember not to let any strangers know that you are home alone. If the phone rings and it is someone you don't know, pretend that your mum or dad are busy. Don't say that you are home alone.

Never give out your address over the phone, unless it is to someone you know in person, and trust.

What Would you do?

You are home alone and there is a knock at the door. You are not expecting anyone. Do you:

(a) open the door;
(b) ignore it;
(c) tell the caller you are not allowed to open the door?

Turn to page 47 for the answer.

ALCOHOL AND SUBSTANCE ABUSE

Alcohol, drugs and solvents all have the potential to seriously damage our health. But that's not the only way they put us at risk. The chemicals in these substances affect the brain's ability to make rational decisions and assess risk effectively. This can lead to some dangerous situations.

The sweet flavour of many alcopops disguises their alcoholic content.

Short-term dangers

Getting drunk or taking a drug such as Ecstasy may seem like part of 'growing up' but even if you only do it once you are taking serious risks. A single beer or an alcopop or a cannabis joint is enough to make a child or young person vomit because young bodies are still developing. Loss of balance, blurred vision and irrational behaviour are common symptoms, making accidents much more likely. Sometimes people experience a heightened sense of aggression or invincibility. Consuming an excessive amount of alcohol can cause death through blood poisoning.

What Would you do?

A family friend offers you a ride home from a party in their car. You know they have been drinking. Do you:

(a) get in the car because you need the lift;

(b) get in the car because you don't want to seem rude;

(c) find a reason not to get into the car?

Turn to page 47 for the answer.

Long-term effects

Alcohol and illegal drugs such as heroin all have serious long-term effects. They are addictive, which means that you become dependent on them and feel you cannot manage without them. Addiction makes you vulnerable in all sorts of ways. As well as health problems such as organ failure, it can lead to mental illness, or involvement in criminal gangs quick to take advantage of someone else's weakness.

Saying 'No'

It can be very difficult to say 'No' to a friend or an older person offering you drugs or alcohol. Telling them you don't need artificial stimulants to have a good time can help you take control, but if you are really under pressure then make up an excuse like 'I'm allergic to alcohol'. They probably won't want to risk the possibility that you might throw up all over them!

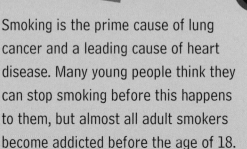

It's a Fact

Smoking is the prime cause of lung cancer and a leading cause of heart disease. Many young people think they can stop smoking before this happens to them, but almost all adult smokers become addicted before the age of 18.

DON'T KEEP IT A SECRET

Children are expected to trust adults. They look to adults to keep them safe. One of the most difficult things for a child or young person to deal with is when an adult – sometimes a relative or close family friend – abuses this trust.

Abuse

If you fall over and hurt yourself, you probably tell your parents. If someone in your class is being mean to you, you may tell your teacher. And if you see someone being mugged, you almost certainly call the police. But when a trusted adult hurts a young person, telling someone about it can feel very difficult indeed.

Abuse of children and young people takes many different forms. A child may be neglected, left on their own at home for unacceptably long periods, beaten or hit, bullied and intimidated or sexually abused. Any adult inflicting abuse is committing a criminal offence, but such people often rely on the child's fear and shame in order to escape prosecution.

The most important thing for abused children to remember is that it is not their fault.

Abusers often try to make their victims feel guilty or afraid.

It is also vital that they don't give up on adults, but find someone – a teacher, a parent, a youth worker or a neighbour – that they can talk to about what has been happening to them. Alternatively, there are some really good organisations with confidential helplines that children can call if they are too afraid to talk to someone face to face.

WHAT'S THE PROBLEM?

'An adult I know always wants to put his arm around me and cuddle me. Sometimes he kisses me and I don't like it. He doesn't do it when my mum is around. I don't think she would believe me if I told her.'

Trust your instincts. If you feel uncomfortable about the way this adult is behaving, then he needs to stop. Do try to talk to your mum. However, if this doesn't help then talk to a teacher or a school counsellor. You have the right to be listened to, and you have the right to be protected from this kind of disturbing behaviour.

In the meantime, try to avoid being alone with this person. Don't worry about appearing rude – just refuse to go anywhere private with him and if you are left alone in the house with him call an adult neighbour or, if you really feel frightened, call the police.

Witnessing a crime

Sometimes a child or young person witnesses a crime that they feel too frightened to report. It may be a crime committed by a gang, or violence committed by one member of the family against another. The people who answer calls to confidential helplines are experts at offering advice about this kind of problem, too. No child should have to keep this kind of secret. Telling someone is not a betrayal and it may stop more people getting hurt.

Help yourself

Tell someone you trust

Here is a list of people who can help:
- A trusted adult such as a relative, a teacher you know well, your school counsellor or a youth worker.
- The police.
- Your doctor.
- A confidential telephone counselling service such as ChildLine (0800 1111).

Don't keep it to yourself.

THINK AHEAD!

Who have you spoken to about your plans?

Staying safe is about taking responsibility for yourself. You don't need to wrap yourself up in cotton wool, but you do need to think ahead, assess risk carefully, take necessary precautions and know what to do if things go wrong.

Proper risk assessment allows you to push boundaries, set challenges, build your self-esteem and have fun while doing all you can to ensure the safety of yourself and others.

What's right for you?

Imagine you have arranged to cycle to the cinema with two friends. Before you leave home, however, you need to think ahead.

Which of the following do you think is the most important? Which is the least important?

- Make sure your bike tyres are pumped up and your brakes are working.
- Check that your mobile phone is working and has credit on it or that you have change for a payphone.
- Remember to take some money for popcorn.
- Tell a parent or another responsible adult what you are doing and where you are going.

- Put your helmet on.
- Pack a bike lock.
- Check that your bike lights are working.
- Check the time the film ends and think about whether it will be dark by then.
- Plan your route to take account of cycle paths and safer roads.

You will probably agree that many of these decisions depend on your particular circumstances. You have to take lots of different things into account. If it isn't going to be dark by the time the film ends you won't need bike lights. If your friends have phones and bike locks then you can share them, if necessary. But telling someone responsible where you are going and what you are doing is always essential. (And a helmet is more important than popcorn!)

What Would you do?

You get to the cinema and watch the film. It finishes earlier than you expected. One friend invites you back to their house for something to eat. The other friend is happy to do this. Now you have more decisions to make. Do you:

(a) call your parent or carer to let them know about the change of plan;

(b) say you have to go and cycle home alone;

(c) go back to your friend's house without calling your parent or carer because you're not expected home yet anyway?

Turn to page 47 for the answer.

HAVE YOUR SAY

"Sometimes I tell my dad I'm at a friend's house when really I'm in town."

"Staying safe is about being responsible."

Glossary

abuse any kind of deliberate hurt or neglect

addiction when the body craves the chemicals found in drugs and alcohol

asthma a condition affecting the lungs and the ability to breathe

cannabis an illegal drug made from the leaves of the cannabis plant

counsellor someone who is professionally trained to listen and offer advice

Ecstasy an illegal drug – usually in the form of a tablet

environment what is around you

epilepsy a condition which causes fits and blackouts

firewall a safety feature for your computer, protecting you from hackers and other interference

hazard danger

highway code advice for staying safe on roads

IMEI number your mobile phone's unique identification number

mugging an attack on a victim in order to steal from them

paedophile someone who sexually abuses children

premium rate numbers telephone numbers that charge a higher than normal rate each time you use them

risk assessment working out how dangerous something is

solvents chemicals such as paint and glue that affect the brain when they are breathed in

undertow a strong current under the water

vulnerable at risk

Further information

USEFUL ORGANIZATIONS AND WEBSITES

ChildLine
A confidential telephone service for vulnerable children and teenagers to talk about their problems with a trained counsellor. The website offers tips on how to beat the bullies and stay safe.
www.childline.org.uk
Helpline number 0800 1111

www.thinkuknow.co.uk
An interactive website with up-to-date news and advice about all the latest phone and internet technology and how to stay safe. The website has different pages for 8-10s and 11-16s.

www.hedgehogs.gov.uk
Colourful, fun site on road safety with interactive games and personal stories.

www.suzylamplugh.org
Go to 'Campaigns and Community', then 'Personal Safety Quiz' for fun and informative quizzes for both primary and secondary school children.

www.livelifesafe.org.uk
More on personal safety, including 'teach ur mum 2 txt'!

www.firekills.gov.uk/kids/01.htm
Child-friendly games and quizzes about all aspects of fire safety.

BOOKS

Jacqui Bailey, Talk About: Drugs, **Wayland, 2008**

Paul Mason, Know the Facts: Drinking and Smoking, **Wayland, 2008**

Jillian Powell, Emotional Health Issues: Alcohol and Drug Abuse, **Wayland, 2008**

Rachel Lynette, Drugs, Heinemann Library, 2007

WHAT WOULD YOU DO?

Page 7: (a) involves a substantial amount of unknown risk. Is the roof safe, for example? However, fetching a ladder (c) introduces a new risk as ladders themselves can be dangerous. Can you find an adult to supervise the ladder? Abandoning your shoe (b) is definitely the safest option.

Page 11: (a) is extremely dangerous. If the knife connects with the 'live' element of the toaster, you will receive a potentially fatal electric shock. (b) is the safest answer. By turning off the power you are breaking the electric current and there is no danger of receiving an electric shock until the current is switched back on. Answer (c) is safe for you, but have you warned the rest of your family about the danger?

Page 19: The only safe answer is (b). People die on railway tracks. Either they are hit by a speeding train (even though they probably looked first) or they are electrocuted by the live current running along the line. **Never** take the risk.

Page 25: (c) is the safest answer. If it is a genuine promotion, why can't he just give you the voucher there and then? Never give your name and address out to strangers. Even if he has ID and does intend to send you a voucher, he has your personal details and may pass them on to others without your permission.

Page 29: Even if you have to stand up in the full carriage, this is better than getting into a carriage with one person you have never met before. The empty carriage is a risk, too, because someone else may get in when the train leaves the station. Another option would be to make yourself known to the guard before you get on the train. Let them know where you are sitting.

Page 36: None of these answers is safe. If you have given someone your address they may decide to pay you a visit when your parents are NOT at home. Meeting someone in a public place doesn't protect you either, though you could ask a responsible adult to go with you. And how do you know if the picture they send you is really them?

Page 39: Never open the door to strangers unless there is a responsible adult with you. However, if you tell the caller you can't open the door then they know that you are home alone and this could put you at risk. Answer (b), ignoring the caller, is definitely the safest option for you. If they really need to speak to someone in your household they can phone or call back later.

Page 41: This is a tricky situation. However, if you get in the car you are putting yourself at risk from a drunk driver. Don't get in the car. Make up any excuse you like and call your parents or carer. Don't leave until a responsible adult is able to see you home safely.

Page 45: Answers (c) and (b) are both changes to your original plan. Is it safe for you to cycle home alone? Do you know your friend's address? Always call your parent or carer if plans change and you are not going to be where they think you are.

INDEX

Numbers in bold refer to illustrations.